art
for
kids

ADVANCED DRAWING

art
for
kids

ADVANCED DRAWING

KATHRYN TEMPLE

union
square
kids

NEW YORK

union
square
kids

NEW YORK

ISBN 978-1-4549-4560-4 (hardcover)
ISBN 978-1-4549-3696-1 (paperback)

Library of Congress Control Number: 2022018371

For information about custom editions, special sales, and premium purchases,
please contact specialsales@unionsquareandco.com.

Printed in China

Lot #:
2 4 6 8 10 9 7 5 3 1

06/22

unionsquareandco.com

Design by Julie Robine

Image credits appear on page 117

For the loves of my life.

To my partner, Lyme.
And to Palmer, who, at three years old,
reminds me how the creative source works:

"The ocean never leaves . . .
It always comes back to us."

CONTENTS

HOW TO BE THE ARTIST ONLY YOU CAN BE

You are the only you there ever was or ever will be. I wrote this book to help you express your unique artistic vision.

"Advanced Drawing" doesn't mean making the most realistic, painstakingly detailed, "accurate" drawing of your subject. To me, it's all about having the tools, skills, and confidence to bring your vision to life. In order to do that, you need some drawing skills, sure, but you also need to have trust in yourself.

The artist Paul Klee described the artist as a tree. The tree pulls from her experience, her past, her imagination: all the rich stuff deep in the soil that she draws up through her roots. She processes all these images and experiences through her body, her eyes, her mind, through the trunk of the tree. And finally, she expresses them through her outstretched branches into her artwork.

I imagine you already like to draw and already have some basic drawing skills—like how to find the basic shape of things, how to see and draw light and shadow, how perspective works, etc.

We'll be using these tools throughout this book. If you find you want a little more detail about these tools and techniques, you may want to check out my first drawing book, *Art for Kids: Drawing*.

In this book we're taking those concepts to the next level and exploring new tools and techniques to bring your artistic vision out onto the page.

We will explore how to see creatively, how to tap into your one-of-a-kind creative point of view, how to build your cast of characters, how to draw more challenging textures, how to draw different kinds of spaces, how to actualize different types of composition and artistic styles, and, finally, how to bring all these tools together into a single artwork.

LIFE RULES TO DRAW BY (EXTENDED REMIX)

1. **Be YOU: because if you don't, who will?**

   It boggles the mind to think there are billions of people alive right this minute. And out of all of those people, there is only one you. There is art within you that will never exist unless you bring it into the world.

2. **Play, explore, and give yourself permission to make bad art!**

   When we're getting into the next stages of drawing (what we might call the "advanced" stuff), it can be tempting to get more and more serious about our art-making. It's important to do the opposite: play is what keeps us growing. In order to learn and grow and discover, we must feel safe to try new things and *not* know what we're doing.

3. **Practice AND stop trying so hard.**

   Practice is an essential part of drawing and being an artist. Just as with sports, or dance, or music, you have to practice in order to build skills. But it's just as important to loosen up and let your instincts take over. This dance—between effort and release—is key to so many things in life, including drawing.

4. **Embrace your "weird."**

   Did you know one of the original meanings of the word *weird* is "magical"? The things that might make you feel different or strange are probably some of the things that make you the most interesting. Let your weirdness soar and find its rightful place in your artwork!

5. **Love your imperfections and limitations.**

   Some artists who have contributed amazing beauty to the world did it, not because of what they were so good at, but because of what they were pretty bad at. We can't all be great at everything. Our artistic "shortcomings" can help define our unique style.

6. **Don't worry about what other people think.**

   This applies for bad *and good* feedback. You may have a few "prize" drawings that everyone says are "so good!" Try not to listen! It's a trap. If we get too invested in what other people think about our art, we may stop branching out and allowing ourselves to "fail" and try new things. Making "bad" drawings that we may objectively think are ugly and terrible is an important part of being an artist. Without experimentation, we'll never truly be ourselves or discover anything new. We'll just be stuck in the trap of trying to make "good" drawings and doing things "right."

MATERIALS AND BASICS

When I was a kid, I didn't always have the nicest art store drawing supplies, so I drew a lot of pictures on the blank backs of junk mail and in the margins of printed pieces of paper with a regular old pencil or a ballpoint pen. Many of the drawings in this book are made with a simple, everyday number 2 (HB) pencil. If you have a number 2 pencil and a piece of paper, you can make incredible art.

Some great art supplies can be found at the drugstore or grocery store, or in a pencil cup in your house! A number 2 pencil (HB) is my favorite. It's not too hard, not too soft, and, like all pencils, sensitive to touch. You want a light line? Press softly. You want a dark line? Bear down. If you need to make darker darks, a black colored pencil can work great.

Pencil Sharpeners

When I'm on the go, I use a simple drugstore pencil sharpener. In the studio, I use an electric sharpener I got at a thrift store.

Erasers

- Vinyl
- Kneaded
- End-of-pencil: you can't really argue with the design of a number 2 pencil! Make marks with one end, erase them with the other!

Pencils

These pencils are from the art supply store. They all have a letter and a number. The letter lets you know how hard (H) or soft (B) the lead is. Harder pencils make lighter marks, and softer pencils make darker marks. The number lets you know the intensity of the pencil. So an 8H would be extremely hard and make very light marks. An 8B would be extremely soft and make very dark, almost black marks.

Paper

Printer Paper: Smooth, lightweight.
Sketch Paper: A little thicker, still pretty smooth.
Drawing Paper: A little heavier, or thicker still. More of a "tooth" or texture on the surface.
Toned Paper: Mid-gray or mid-brown paper that can be fun for using dark and white pencils.

With all of these, I try to find recycled paper, or paper made from sustainably harvested trees whenever possible.

I drew the left figure with drugstore supplies. I drew the right one using art store supplies.

CHAPTER 1 SEEING WITH YOUR IMAGINATION

SEEING BEYOND WHAT'S THERE

No one else has ever seen the world exactly the way you do. To make art unique to you, you don't have to try super hard or come up with something groundbreaking. You just need to be yourself. This may require getting quiet, settling in, and allowing yourself to look around and see the world through your eyes. The way *only you can*. What you see, imagine, and make is unique in this world, and there is a special place for it.

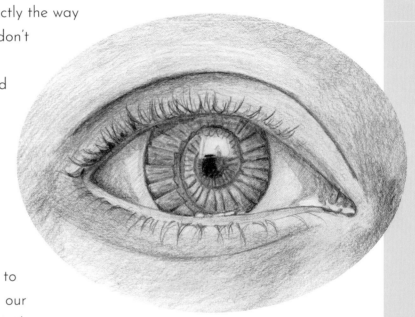

In *Art for Kids: Drawing* we learned to see the world as it is: instead of drawing our "idea" of something, to actually see what's there.

Instead of this:

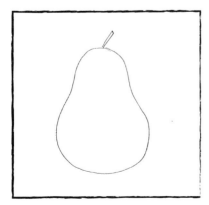

we draw this:

Now, imagine taking that even further. We're also going to see what's there and then step "through" what we see to something else. We're still going to see the world in terms of shape and light and shadow, but now we're also letting our imaginations take a turn to see new things within all those shapes and shadows. This way of looking at the world can provide hours of entertainment: You may see animals in the knots and grain of a wood floor. You may discover surprised monster faces in a faucet or a pile of dirty clothes.

When you open your eyes to this kind of creative seeing, suddenly there are fascinating shapes and light forms and shadows everywhere.

If you tend to take making art very seriously, this can help keep things playful. It can open up possibilities and keep you from getting stuck in the mindset that there's a "right" way to draw.

▲ An ordinary floorboard

Instead of just seeing floorboard, we may see:

or this:

▲ A bunny or a little ▲ penguin chick.

6

WHAT DO YOU SEE?

I love this tree. I call it the "puppy tree," and I see it every time I go on one of my favorite hikes.

See this rain-worn sticker on my trash can? I was on a walk with my daughter and we passed by our trash can at the curb. She said, "Hey look! A duck face!" Can you see it?

What Creatures Live in Your Clothes Pile?

If you tend to be a little messy, you may already have a pile of dirty clothes on the floor. If not, make one. Don't try to arrange anything, just lift a heap of clothes in your arms and drop them on the floor or in the laundry basket. Now: take some time looking at it. Take some time doodling. Do any forms jump out at you? If not that's fine, just keep looking and doodling. It's like exercise. You're making your creative muscles stronger.

 Here's a laundry basket if I simply observe and draw what I see on the surface level.

Here's what I see if I let my eyes relax a little and let my imagination have a little more room to play. Suddenly there's a frog-faced old creature with a fishy beard hanging out in the laundry basket.

Keep your imagination flowing.
Do you see any forms hiding
in this pile of clothes?

What do you see in the rocky form?
Do you see the bear head?

MEET YOUR IMAGINATION MONSTER!

See these people? They're not looking up at the world around them. They're not looking at each other. Each of them has a creative force just begging to come out to make things, to draw, to express something. But first they need to make space.

Every person has a magical force within them that has creative ideas. A force that imagines, daydreams and pieces thoughts together in a way no one else on earth does. Some people call this genius, spark, inspiration. I like to think of it as our imagination monster.

Your imagination is a singular, one-of-a-kind magical animal. A lot of what we learn and are told to do as we grow older tames this magical creature: looking at screens too much (tablets, phones, TVs), or being told to be quiet and still in the middle of a boring class when we want to run, sing, scream, or skip rocks across a pond. When someone yells at us for being messy, when someone says something that hurts our feelings or makes us feel ashamed . . . all these things make that strange, wonderful imagination monster hide deeper and deeper into the shadows of our mind, our spirit. So our job as artists is to do things that coax our imagination out to play. Things that give our imagination the message—no matter what anyone else is saying—that we respect it and welcome it and that it's safe to come out of hiding to play and to create art with us.

▶ How to let your imagination monster come out of hiding

The imagination monster only comes out to play if it feels welcome.

There are some things that discourage your imagination monster from coming out to stretch its legs: too much busyness, trying to be perfect, trying to impress other people.

If you spend a lot of time in front of screens, try cutting down on that time. Next time you feel the urge to watch a video or scroll down a screen, pause. **Let yourself get a little bored instead.** Slowing down and allowing yourself to "do nothing" is one of the best ways to make room for your imagination.

HOW TO SPACE OUT

Here is a simple, silly, step-by-step guide:

1. Sit down and stare into space (out a window, at the wall, whatever, just pick something and stick with it).

2. Notice the overwhelming urge to get up and *actually do something!* AAAGGHH!

3. Override that urge and stay seated, staring into space.

4. Repeat steps 1 to 3 until you finally give in and find your mind wandering all over the place.

PROJECT How to Loosen Up

▼ Try drawing on an already
messed-up surface.

▼ Find an old envelope in the recycling
bin and draw a picture on it.

▼ Draw on a teeny-tiny surface.

▼ Make some "bad" drawings!

Experiment with anything that takes the pressure off and gets
you out of your head. Anything that gets you as far away from
the idea of "perfect" as possible. We aren't perfect, so our art
isn't supposed to be either.

Give Something Little a Little Attention

Open your hand, turn your palm up and stare at it for one full minute.

In case you're thinking "Hey! *We just did this!*" I assure you, this is different from spacing out. When you space out, you're loosening up and letting go of effort of any kind. In this one minute, you're actively giving one small space— the incredible map of lines and creases in the palm of your hand—your full attention. You're noticing, seeing, observing. Spacing out is relaxed, it's passive, it's about unclenching your artistic fist. Attention is active. It requires energy and focus.

We're not going for perfect.
. . . We're going for alive!

Tip

If you're feeling stuck? Get moving.
Though ideas and inspiration may come from your mind, your body/ hand/ arm makes the drawing. It can help to jump around, dance, jiggle, stretch. Physically loosen up. I find sometimes a walk gets my blood flowing and helps shake out the creative cobwebs. Sometimes my best ideas come when I'm just listening to music and moving around.

CHAPTER 2

DRAWING AS A FORM OF SEARCHING

In *Art for Kids: Drawing*, we learned to find the simple shapes inside more complex subjects. By finding the simple shapes, we can draw much more complicated forms.

Once you've got the idea of how to find the simple shapes in things, you can stop trying so hard. With gestural drawing, we're not "breaking things down" into simpler forms as much as we're letting our hand wander and search across the page. The artist Paul Klee said drawing was "taking a line for a walk." To me it feels like dancing.

EXPLORING LOOSE AND GESTURAL DRAWING

Now we're going to make a little mess as we find the shape of something. We're going to leave a record of our journey . . . without feeling like we need to hide our track marks. Or make the drawing look like it dropped magically from the sky.

When I was first learning to draw, I placed a ton of importance on "getting it right." Making it look as much like the thing I was drawing as I possibly could. Making sure it didn't have a bunch of "mistakes." If there were loose lines or distortions, I always wanted to "fix" them.

Here's the secret though: THERE IS NO SUCH THING AS PERFECT! We don't want to be cameras! Everyone has a camera in their pocket these days. You are so much cooler than a camera! You are wild. You're alive. You're gloriously imperfect.

See this tree? I circled and arced and swirled my line to feel the roundness of the trunk and the branches, almost like my hand had X-ray vision and could see straight through to the back of the tree while I was drawing it. The curved lines that follow the round shape of the trunk are called contour lines. I chose to use a big fat marker so that my lines would have to be bold and permanent. It's hard to make a timid line with a bright marker.

It took me a long time to realize that trying to make something perfect can squeeze the life out of it.

HOW TO TAKE A LINE FOR A WALK

1.

2.

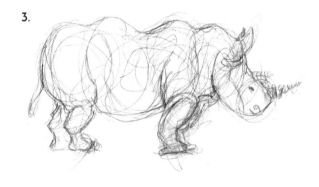

3.

If this step-by-step feels funny to you, that makes sense! There are millions of ways to find your way through a subject like this with your pencil. Your natural searching process will look different from mine. I'm showing you the journey *my* hand took just to give you a sense of what a loose and wandering drawing can feel like. It's all about getting out of your head and letting your intuition take over. The final drawing doesn't really matter. The searching is the point.

Give your hand permission to meander around. Let yourself be squiggly, wiggly, bold, weird.

Now that you've seen one way to search for form, try taking your own line for a walk.

17

▶ **Try This**

If I'd been drawing a real animal, the
drawing would be even less precise.
Drawing a subject in motion is
a great way to explore loosening up in your drawings. It's
nearly impossible to "capture"
the subject's precise likeness,
so instead you're making a sort of
record of movement. If you have
a cat or a dog, or a friend
or sibling who would be
willing to model for you,
see if you can draw them
moving around. Or see
if you can draw an adult
in your life putting the groceries
away or doing the dishes.

▶ Loose, Expressive Drawing from a Photo

You can also draw in this style from a photograph. If you're trying to capture a particular pose or gesture in a drawing, a photo can be really helpful.

You may want to make all your drawings this way, and you may not. Some artists (I'm one of them, despite my affection for wild, free drawing) naturally tend toward a tighter, more realistic style of drawing . . . and we'll explore different styles throughout the rest of this book. But learning to let go and be free can help you get better at those other styles too. It opens you up to an experience of discovery you may not have had before.

CREATING A CAST OF CHARACTERS

When I'm drawing, I think of all my subjects as characters. Even if I'm drawing a marble or a spool of thread, I think of that object as a character that is alive on my page and alive in the space that I've created for it.

Some artists find themselves struggling to think of things to draw. Even when I taught college students, I can't tell you how many times I heard "I love to draw, but I get stuck and can't think of what to draw."

When I draw, I draw some from memory, some from imagination, and some from direct observation—where I look at a thing or a person and draw what I see. When I draw from observation, I like to use all different kinds of "source materials": objects, people, and photographs.

This chapter is designed to help you develop a cast of characters from all different kinds of source materials. When you've got a cast of characters to draw from, you always have go-to subjects when you're ready to create. These projects and exercises will help you build your visual "vocabulary" so you'll have more tools at your fingertips to bring the pictures in your mind out onto the page.

CREATE A CAST OF BASIC SHAPES— BUILDING BLOCKS OF A WORLD

Let's start out with a handful of the most basic shapes: a tube, a sphere, a cube, a rectangular box, a cone, and a paper ribbon. It's great to have models of these simple shapes available to work from and you can create them from basic objects you find around your house or in the recycling bin.

If you can get a grasp on these basic shapes, you can draw just about anything. When you're drawing something from your imagination that's built of these basic shapes, you can use your shape "models" to see how light falls across them and casts shadows across the surface they're sitting on. This is one of my favorite tricks I've learned from years of making art: you can draw from your imagination AND from life to create really fascinating images. Your imagination allows you to draw things that may not even exist in real life, and by adding detail and shadow through observation of an actual object, you can make your imagined drawing feel even more "real."

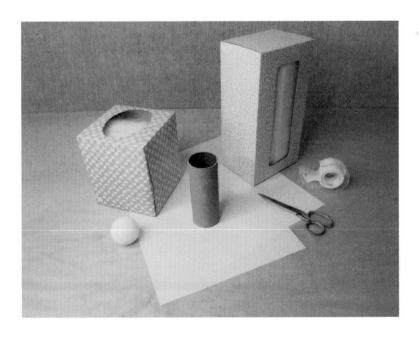

Here I've gathered a toilet-paper tube, a Ping-Pong ball, a square box, and a rectangular tissue box. I'll also need some plain white paper, tape, and scissors to make the cone and to wrap my boxes. I'm using a Ping-Pong ball that's already white, but you can also paint an old ball white. By making all these shapes white, it makes it much easier to see (and draw) all the different shades of gray in the lights and shadows.

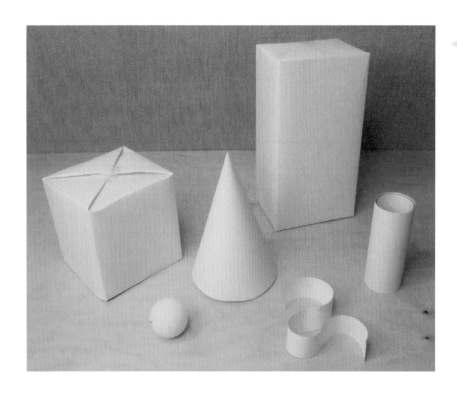

And here they are "all dressed up" and ready to model for your creations!

DRAWING YOUR CAST OF BASIC SHAPES

The steps for all these shapes are basically the same.

1. Find your basic shapes.

2. Erase extra lines.

3. Identify your light source and find your mid-tone shadows.

4. Find your darker shadows and lighter grays. (I like to keep from going too dark at this stage so I can darken them up later once I have a sense of the full range of gray tones.)

5. Find your lightest shadows, and darken your darker tones as you see the relationships of dark to light become clearer. Finally, draw the cast shadow. (Notice the range of lights and darks even in the cast shadow.)

Once you've got a sense of how to draw these basic shapes, practice drawing them at different angles: lay your tube down at an angle, or set one of the boxes high up on a shelf so you're looking at it from below.

PRACTICE DRAWING STAIRS

I've always loved drawing stairs. I like how angular and three-dimensional they are. I like how light falls on them in such dramatic ways. I like how it's fairly simple to create the illusion of depth in a drawing with stairs.

One simple way to practice stairs is to cut a long narrow sheet of paper (say 3 x 11 inches or so) and do an accordion fold, like this.

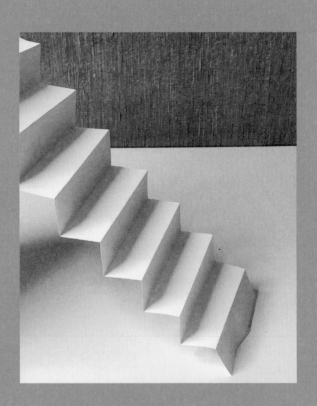

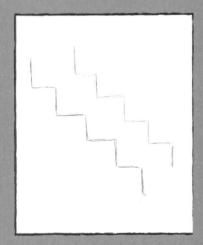

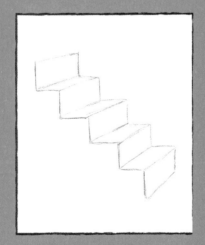

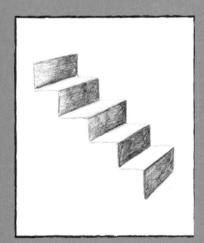

MAKE COMPLEX FORMS WITH BASIC SHAPES

When you have a handle on these basic shapes, you can put them together to make all kinds of cool things. Rectangular boxes can be a city of skyscrapers! A tissue box and toilet paper rolls can become a towering medieval castle!

DRAWING YOUR OWN SIMPLIFIED FIGURE

Some artists feel intimidated about drawing the human figure. It can be liberating not to feel like you have to painstakingly study the human figure every time you want a person in your drawing. I have several different versions of people I draw from my imagination, and I'll just sketch them mindlessly into a drawing without thinking too much about it. I want to give you some tools so you can find your version of a simple little figure you can place into whatever scene you dream up.

▶ Simple Figure: Basic Shapes Method

1. First, draw a ball for the head, a cone for the torso/dress, and tubes for the arms and legs.

2. Next, sketch in some circular shapes for the hands and toes of the shoes.

3. Then use some simple horizontal lines (that curve like a slight smile) to mark the eyes (halfway down the ball), the nose, and the mouth. Imagine where the light source is (mine is in the upper right, shining down on the subject), and start to lightly sketch in some shadows on the left side.

4. Finally, add simple hair and more detail in the eyes, hands, and feet. Using everything we learned about how light and shadow falls across simple shapes earlier, draw more shadows on the figure.

▶ Simplified Figure: Quick, Sketchy Lines Method

If I want to sketch a figure in a setting, an easy way to do it is just using some very basic lines. I pretty much only used an oval and some slightly curved lines to draw this figure.

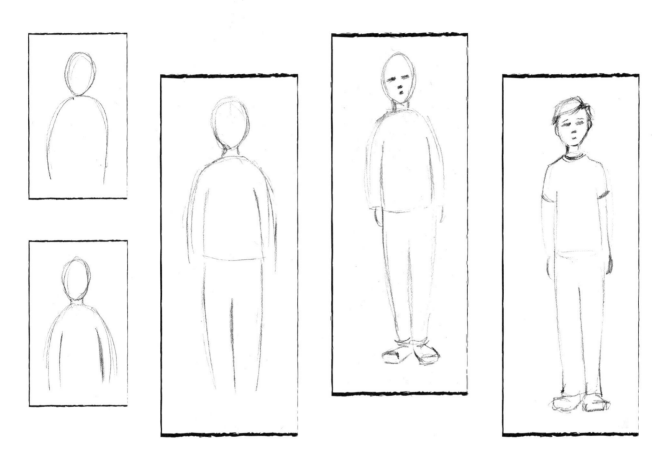

If you want more detail about the basics of how to draw faces and bodies, you can explore the faces and bodies chapters in *Art for Kids: Drawing* (pages 76–101). In those chapters, we cover the basics of facial shapes and proportions in the "face map" and the fundamentals of drawing the human body.

And if you find a photo of a face or body you want to capture *exactly* instead of just getting a feel for, like the drawings here, you can use the gridding technique we explore in Chapter 7.

USING A PHOTO AS A REFERENCE FOR A MORE DETAILED FIGURE

For this drawing, I specifically wanted to draw someone who was reading a text, because it reminds me of the same pose in lots of old paintings where a figure is reading a letter (written on a piece of paper). Even though this is a common gesture most of us see in the people around us every day, there's something lovely and delicate about this pose, and I wanted to capture it in a drawing. I chose this photo because I like this person's body language, facial expression, and the way the light falls over their hands and body.

1. First loosely sketch the head shape, the curve that marks the centerline of the figure's face, the horizontal curve that marks the eyeline, and little lines to mark the bottom of the nose and the mouth.

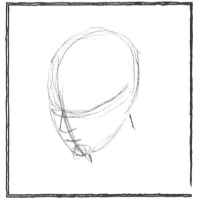

2. Next add a little definition to the nose, chin, and
browline. Next define the
lips and eyes. Also mark
the neckline and hairline.

3. Now it's time to get a better
sense of the whole figure:
block in the arms and the
edges of the clothes and
hands.

4. At this point I checked in with myself to see what's really most important to me to capture. I'm not trying to draw a portrait. I'm referencing this photo to capture a particular feeling. I'm not interested in the glasses, so I used my imagination to fill in the rest of the eyes. The gesture, stance, and hands are most important to me.

5. Add some initial shading to the face, hair, and body of the figure. Notice how the light source is coming from the upper left of the picture so the darker shadows are on the right. Add further definition to the clothes.

6. Now use a softer, darker pencil (I used a 2B) to get some more medium darks and darker darks. I made tiny circles with my pencil to capture the feel of the tiny curls of hair. Notice how the hair is darker at the hairline and the back of the head, farther away from the light source. Use your number 2 to add more mid-tones to the skin and clothes.

7. Now add your final details. Add depth by darkening some shadows. Use your eraser to "pull" any highlights (I used mine on the figure's forehead).

USING PHOTOS FOR CHARACTERS IN YOUR DRAWINGS

When drawing a human or human-like figure (like an imaginary extraterrestrial being or a superhero), referencing photos can be very helpful. You can use the photo as a jumping-off place for the figure. It doesn't have to be an exact portrait or even really look at all like the original person photographed.

For all of these drawings, I looked to photos I liked for reference. I chose the photos because there was something about the figure's face or bodily gesture that interested me.

I'm purposefully omitting a lot of detail. Sometimes even a really simplified, not particularly realistic figure can be very emotionally expressive. Just the particular curve of the shoulders or tilt of the head can communicate as much or more than a highly detailed portrait could.

CHAPTER 4
EXPLORING ADVANCED TEXTURES

Once you've begun developing a cast of characters, there are many ways you can bring your subjects to life. Paying close attention to the texture of the subject you're drawing can give your pictures more dimension and depth.

In this chapter, we're going to explore how to use your pencil(s) to create a range of different surface textures. There are some surface textures that seem so magical and complex that some artists avoid them altogether. We're going to strip away the mystery and tackle those more challenging surfaces.

▶ Textile

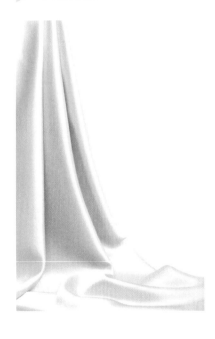

1. First, find the basic shape of your draped fabric, including some of the lines of the inner folds.

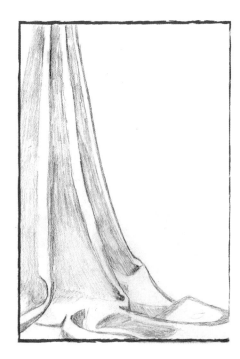

2. Find more details in the folds of the fabric. Sketch the shapes of some of the shadows. Notice where the highlights are that you'll leave white.

3. Begin to sketch in the medium grays for the dark and medium shadows.

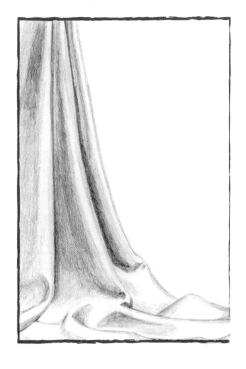

4. Add the darkest shadows and the lighter grays. Pay attention to the transitions between tones to capture the satiny sheen of this fabric.

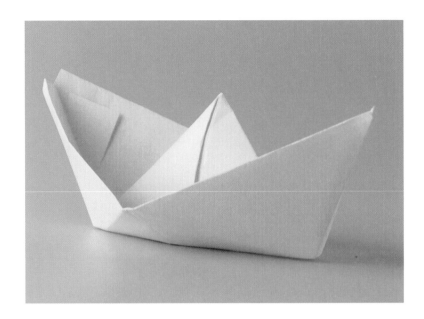

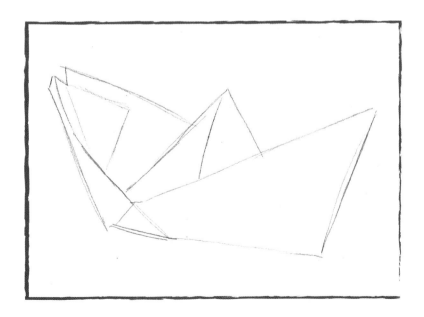

1. Find the basic shape of the paper boat. It is mostly made up of different shaped triangles and straight lines.

2. Sketch in the medium gray tones. At this step I noticed some details I didn't see the first time: like an additional fold line along the bottom right of the boat. Also a little crinkle on the right side of the middle triangle of the boat.

3. Now sketch in the lighter gray tones. And keep looking for details you may not have seen on your first or second glance. Add some of these small details (like little creases along the upper left edge, or lines in the center fold in the middle of the boat) with slightly darker marks.

4. Go back over your medium tones again and make them darker and richer. Darken your lighter grays where needed. Draw the cast shadow on the surface where the boat sits. Draw the dark gray line where the bottom of the boat meets the table.

5. Using your number 2 pencil, continue to refine details and adjust the relationships between shadows. Finally, darken your darkest darks. I used a 2B pencil to darken the shadow where the boat sits and to darken some of the darkest creases and folds in the paper.

► Glass

Glass is a fun challenge because it's clear. It forces us to really search for the odd shapes of light and shadow. I chose to draw a glass with water in it because I love to look at light passing through water.

1. Find the basic shapes. Here we've got three ellipses (a kind of slightly flattened oval): the top and bottom of the glass, and the ellipse for the surface of the water. Connect the top and bottom shapes with straight lines and find the cast shadow shape.

2. Search for the shapes of the darks and lights in the glass, the water and the cast shadow. You'll need your artist eyes for this because these shapes are different for every glass of water.

3. Fill in some of the mid-tone grays. You'll start to get a feel for the water and the light passing through the glass. Now sketch in the lighter grays. Even though this is a very light drawing—very white-on-white-looking—there are in fact very few true whites—where just the untouched paper shows through.

4. Now draw in some of your darker darks. If you're using only a number 2 pencil, press down harder for these. If you're using another darker pencil (like a 4B or a black colored pencil), now is the time to use that pencil.

5. Now go back in and make your lighter grays a little richer, a little darker.

6. I went back over the light grays in the glass and also laid down a layer of light gray across the background. Laying down the background gray is very important because it makes our highlights in the glass really pop. Now add your final darkest darks to the glass, the water, and the cast shadow.

▶ Metal/ Reflective

1. Find the basic shapes: two ellipses for the top and the bottom of the can and then, for now, straight lines to connect the sides. This can has a fantastic wavy texture. There are sixteen curved lines that follow the same curve of the top and bottom of the can.

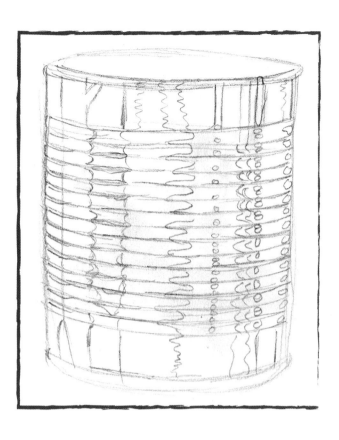

2. Draw the curved lines and then go up and down the sides of the can to make the little "C" shaped curves for each line. Go ahead and mark the basic shapes of shadows and highlights.

3. Now begin to sketch in the middle grays in the reflections and shadows on the can. Notice how under each little curved rib on the can there is a shadow.

4. Now it's time to find the darker darks. I used a 2B pencil, but you could either bear down harder with your number 2 or use a black colored pencil.

5. Continue developing your mid-grays and your darks. Also, find the cast shadow on the table. I found that my can reflected light onto the table at the lower left below the can. Also, block in values for the table and background. In my case, it was a dark gray table and a very light gray for the background.

▶ Fluffy Clouds

This is a fun way to create fluffy, cotton-candy clouds. Clouds have no hard edges; they're constantly moving and shifting. They are simply droplets of water suspended in air. Instead of laying the shapes down with pencil, we're going to lay down a gray "ground" on our paper and then "pull" the shape of the cloud with an eraser. Then we'll work back in with pencil to deepen the shadows.

1. Use the side of your pencil to "tone" the sky gray. I used a soft pencil. Shade darker at the top of the page and get lighter as you move toward the bottom of your paper.

2. Rub with a clean rag to smooth out the pencil marks in your sky.

3. Use your end-of-pencil eraser to draw the circles and curves that make up the basic cloud shape.

4. Identify your light source. Here, the sun is coming from the upper right corner of the
    page. Keep lifting the light areas of the cloud with your eraser. I'm making tiny circular
    motions as I erase so that I don't have any hard lines. Just soft, puffy cloud.

5. Now work back and forth between light and shadow with your eraser and your soft
    pencil. If you want to smooth out your pencil marks, use your rag to rub them smooth.

6.   Next, add a few mid tones and edges with your number 2 pencil.

1. First, find the basic shapes of the puppy. She's made up of lots of circles, ovals, and curves.

2. Shape up the details of the puppy's body. Then, take some time sketching in areas of value. I'm starting with some of the darker patches of her fur. She's a black puppy, but her fur has a range of values: all the way from the darkest black to white highlights. Notice the direction of the fur's growth. Draw your pencil marks in the same direction the fur grows.

3. You are basically drawing a little map for yourself to follow as you continue to develop the fur texture on your puppy. Focus on the medium and dark areas. Continue to make your pencil marks in the direction the fur grows. I am still using a number 2 pencil at this point. I know I will go darker in these areas eventually.

4. Start layering in your light and mid-gray fur lines. You may find more dark areas you want to layer in. Use your eraser to lighten your shape lines from your initial sketch. See how there are no hard lines in this puppy? Every part of her body has fuzzy soft edges. Now go back in and replace those hard lines with fuzzy little fur marks.

5. Now it's time to get out your darker pencil: I used a 2B for this step. This puppy has some really rich blacks in her fur. Start sketching them in on the darkest areas under her ears and on her chest and front legs. Go back and forth between your number 2 pencil and your darker pencil to get the transitions right between dark black and gray. This is what's going to make the fur look velvety and less scruffy. Give her eyes some attention, darkening the pupils and leaving the bright white highlights.

6. In this final step, make the dark blacks as rich and deep as you can. I used an 8B pencil. I also kept my 2B and number 2 handy so that I could continue to adjust my medium grays and make changes to the transitions between light and dark. When you spend a lot of time on a drawing, you may find you see more subtle differences in value the longer you look at your subject.

You may need to sharpen your pencil frequently. Making all these tiny marks can make it dull quickly.

▶ Try This

Now that you've learned how to draw all these fun and satisfying textures, try mixing it up. Take one of the textures and apply it to a totally incompatible object.

The artist Meret Oppenheim made sculptures with shocking textures that jarred the senses: she famously covered an actual teacup, saucer and spoon with fur! ▶

▶ Try This

Check out this image! It has three complex surface textures in one picture: silky fur, shiny metal, and splashing water. Can you give it a try?

CHAPTER 5 CREATING A SPACE

Now that you've gotten a sense of how to create a cast of characters, you need a place to put them.

See how this character is just floating on the page surrounded by emptiness? You may want to draw all your characters this way, or you may want to ground them into a particular place. In this chapter, we're going to focus on different ways to create a space for your characters to "live" in. You may want them to exist in a simple space with just a little bit of shadow. You may want them inside a replica of your apartment or house. You may want them in a vast landscape, or in a dreamscape of futuristic vehicles in a highway of clouds.

Creating "space" or "ground" can be as simple as drawing a horizontal line across your paper and adding some shading to suggest a floor and a wall and casting a shadow to ground them in this space.

You also don't have to have any characters in your spaces. The spaces themselves can be the central subject of your drawings: it's all up to you.

Staring into the Corner

This is a great, simple way to create a space from direct observation for your characters to occupy. Take a few minutes looking at the corner of a room. Position yourself so you're looking at the corner straight-on—so you're in the middle of the room and there's about as much wall to your right and your left as you look at the corner. A corner is composed of such simple shapes: basically one "Y" and an upside down "Y." (If you're having a hard time "seeing it," check out the colored overlays on the photo below. See how the orange "Y" marks the ceiling and upper walls and the upside-down pink "Y" marks the floor and lower walls?) Each surface: the walls, ceiling, and floor are all different values or gradations of value.

See how each flat surface (wall, ceiling or floor) is a different value? And how there's a little variation of value on each surface?

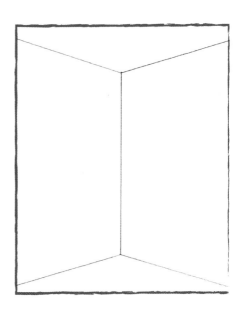

1. Draw your corner by finding your "Y" shape and your upside down "Y" shape.

2. Squint to see if you can see the different values more clearly. What area is the darkest? The lightest? To me, the left wall looks like a mid-tone and the right wall a lighter gray. Begin sketching in these values.

3. Now add your lighter grays (the ceiling) and darker grays (the floor).

4. Do you see how the left wall is darker where it meets the top edge of the corner and the ceiling? And then it is a lighter gray as it moves to the left? The right wall is also a little darker in the upper edge of the corner. Move through your drawing to find these subtle variations in value.

You can keep it simple like this or add as much architectural detail as you want.

In this corner exercise, two-point perspective is in play. If you're interested in exploring the concept of linear perspective (one-point, two-point, and three-point perspective) turn to page 112.

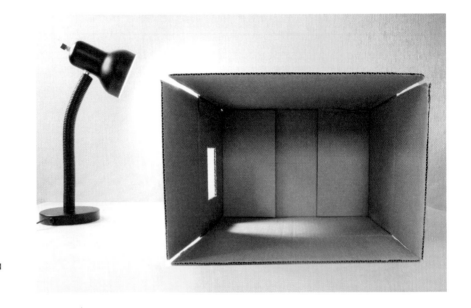

Here's a trick I use sometimes in the studio if I want to get a sense of how light falls through a room. I set up a miniature version of the space I imagine in my mind.

You'll need a box (like a shoebox or a shipping box), scissors, and a light source (a little clamp light, a table lamp, or natural light coming through a window).

First, build your room: draw where you want the windows or doors and use scissors to cut out the shapes. The lines can be imperfect and jagged; you can straighten them out in your drawing as much as you want. This is just to get a sense of how light falls in this space.

Now place your box room on a table (or floor) and set up your light source.

Later, you can place "characters" and objects in the room to represent the scene you imagine. I obviously can't put a real person in this tiny room, but I can put a figurine in there as a stand-in. It will give me an idea of how the light falls over the figure and how the figure takes up/ lives in the space.

BOX ROOM DRAWING

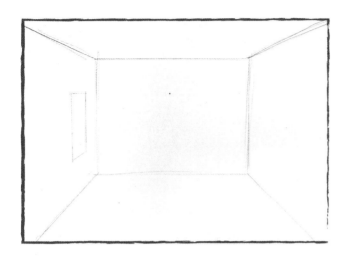

1. Draw the back wall of your room. Draw the diagonal lines that mark the floor and side walls. (This room follows the rules of one-point perspective; if you want, you can draw your horizon and vanishing point, or you can "eyeball it" like I'm doing). Now draw the window on the left wall.

2. Sketch the shape of the light cast across the floor from the window. Begin sketching in some of your mid-gray shadows on the walls and floor.

3. Now darken up your darkest areas. In this room, they're on the wall with the window and on the floor just below the window. There are also sharp dark lines marking the edges of the room. Also find the light grays on the outer edge of the bright light cast across the floor.

EXTERIOR SPACES

▶ Drawing "scapes": landscapes, cityscapes, and imaginationscapes

Another kind of space your figures can live in is an outdoor space. This can be a traditional landscape, a cityscape or even an eerie imagined space. You can use different source materials—the world around you, a miniature model, or a photograph—to create these spaces.

Landscapes

If you live in the country, you might have a beautiful farm or mountain view right out your front door. If you live in a city or town, you might have to get a little more creative to find a landscape to draw.

▶ Messy bed landscape

If you're like me, you may not make your bed every morning. Now you've got a great artistic excuse to leave your pillows and blankets rumpled and askew.

To the untrained eye, this probably just looks like a messy bed. But if we're looking creatively, we may see all kinds of landscape opportunities. I'm imagining the pillows, blanket and sheet as mountains, hills, and a winding river. I'm using observation and my imagination to draw this landscape.

1. Find the basic shapes of your messy bed landscape: the hills, the curves of the river.

2. Next, notice how the light falls over the pillows and blankets. Add shadows where you think they help define your landscape. Leave out any details you don't want.

3. Now I'm looking at the sheet and seeing which folds help create a sense of river water running downstream.

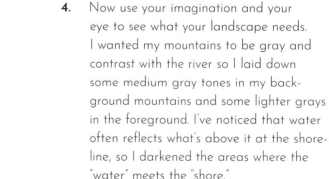

I've pretty much stopped looking at the bed at this point and I'm looking at my drawing and using my imagination and instincts to make my drawing choices.

4. Now use your imagination and your eye to see what your landscape needs. I wanted my mountains to be gray and contrast with the river so I laid down some medium gray tones in my background mountains and some lighter grays in the foreground. I've noticed that water often reflects what's above it at the shoreline, so I darkened the areas where the "water" meets the "shore."

DRAW A LANDSCAPE FROM A PHOTO

I chose this photo to draw from because it has a lot of elements I'm naturally drawn to: it has one-point perspective (the lines of the country road and trees all come together in the deep background at the vanishing point), it has puddles that reflect light and trees in a way that feels magical to me, and it is framed on both sides by towering trees that remind me of the tubes we drew in Chapter 3.

1. Sketch in your basic geometric shapes. The path is an upside-down triangle. Find the largest tree shapes that line the road. Do you see how the trees get smaller (thinner and shorter) the farther away they are?

2. Sketch in the more organic (curving and natural) lines along the road for the dirt and leaves along the path's edges. Sketch in puddles along the path.

3. Sketch in the smaller trees in the background. Start adding value and depth to your drawing. When I squint, I notice the lightest parts of the image are the little triangle of light at the end of the road and the spots on the road that are wet, reflecting the light of the sky.

4. Continue adding detail and value. Sketch in the smaller, lighter gray trees. Add the medium grays along the road and in the puddles. The darkest areas are at different spots on the largest trees in the foreground.

5. Develop the medium gray trees in the background. The edges of these smaller trees are also softer than those of the big trees. Draw the reflected trees in the puddles. Continue to circle through your drawing, adding final details and darkest darks.

DRAW A CITYSCAPE

Maybe you live in an apartment building in a city and all you have to do is look out your window for inspiration. If so, for the next project, you can set your chair and drawing paper up next to the window and start observing and drawing. If not, you can construct a model cityscape or work from a photo.

▶ Make a Cityscape

Here you can go back to your cast of basic shapes to create a city scape. Boxes will represent buildings. If you need more shapes, go back around the house or in the recycling bin and see what you can find: cereal boxes, tissue boxes, etc. can all be great stand-ins for skyscrapers.

▶ Draw Your Cityscape!

1. Draw a horizon line. I placed mine about a third of the way up from the bottom of the paper. Now draw a vertical line that crosses over the horizon line. It represents the edge of the closest building.

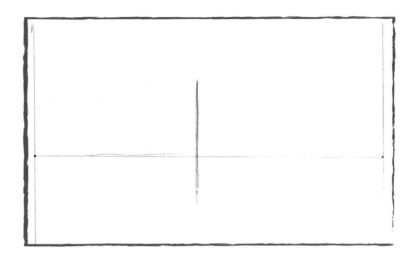

2. Start sketching in the tops, bottoms, and sides of that first building. (If you want to use two-point perspective, draw your two vanishing points at either side of your horizon line). The tops and bottoms of all the buildings will angle toward the vanishing points. Draw the back vertical edges of the building.

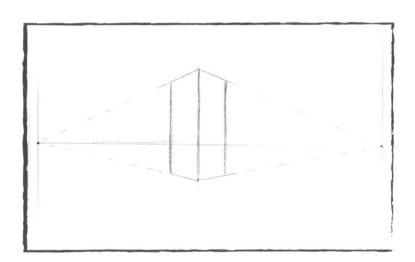

3. Continue drawing the next buildings back as you move back in the space, deeper into the picture.

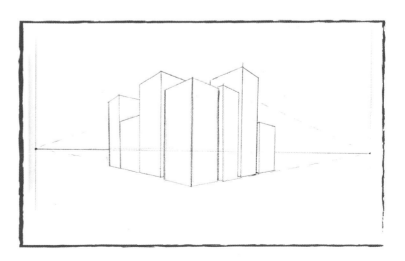

4. Now notice where your light source is and how the right sides of the buildings are in shadow and how they cast shadow across the right side of the space.

5. Finally, add imagined detail to your buildings and to their surroundings—adding lines and shadows to create sidewalks and streets.

Imaginationscapes

Imaginationscapes are spaces that don't exist in the outside world but are born from your imagination. Maybe you imagine a vast expanse with a checkered floor and a tree growing out of it. Maybe a staircase leads to a door in the tree and puffy clouds float in the distance. You can piece different source materials together to make these mysterious spaces come to life. More on that in Chapter 10.

CHAPTER 6

CONSTRUCTING YOUR DRAWING: COMPOSITION

"Composition" can seem really abstract and complex, but it boils down to something pretty simple: it's how you arrange (or compose) the parts of your picture on the page.

Some artists don't consciously think about the "rules" of composition at all. They just start moving their pencil around and working it out by instinct. This is a wonderful way to create. I draw this way most of the time—especially when I'm sketching and brainstorming ideas. But sometimes, if my picture feels a little "off" and I can't figure out why, I can use some of the tools of composition to see if I can make it work better.

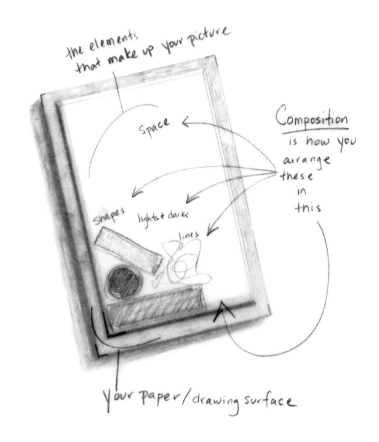

the elements that make up your picture

Space

Composition is how you arrange these in this

shapes lights + darks

lines

Your paper/drawing surface

Here's one of endless ways I could have composed those basic elements into a complete picture.

FORMAT

The first composition choice you make is about the shape and orientation of your paper. The most common shape is a rectangle (I work on a rectangle most of the time) but you may also choose a square, a circle, or some other shape. And then you decide how to orient your paper: horizontally (flatter, like a landscape) or vertically (taller, like a portrait).

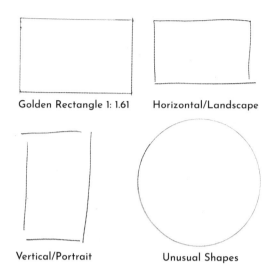

Golden Rectangle 1: 1.61   Horizontal/Landscape

Vertical/Portrait   Unusual Shapes

▶ Rule of Thirds

The rule of thirds is a simple, but really useful way to create a balanced composition. Start by dividing your paper into thirds from side to side and again from top to bottom.

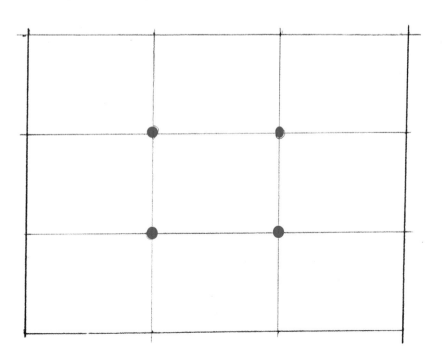

For hundreds of years artists have understood that using these lines as a guide to organize the elements of their artwork helped create a balanced, pleasing composition. The four points where the lines intersect (the pink dots) are considered powerful areas to place your main subject, or focal point. If you look at the second composition on the next page, with the cloud and figure, it's organized according to the rule of thirds. See how the horizon line is at the bottom third? And how the figure is standing at one of these magic points of intersection?

▶ Let's Begin Exploring

We're starting with a horizontal rectangle for our drawing surface. Let's say you've decided you want to draw a picture of a cloud, a figure, and a simple, empty landscape. Even with only three basic elements, you have endless options about how to compose your picture. The way you compose your drawing can affect how your artwork *makes the viewer feel*.

There are a million ways to do this beautifully! (And also a million ways to do it that don't work so well.) For example:

In this first composition, the person is in the center of the frame. I drew the cloud right above the figure and drew the horizon line between the two. This composition doesn't work very well: the cloud is so close to the edge of the paper that it draws your eye to the top instead of into the picture. It also feels like I ran out of room on the page. The horizon line feels less like a distant horizon and more like a random line just sitting on top of the person's head.

Now look at this next one. I've drawn the horizon line about one-third up from the bottom of the page. I've given my cloud some room to breathe. I've placed the figure to the right of center and drawn the body so that it overlaps the horizon line and the cloud in the background. Overlapping elements can create a sense of depth.

Let's try making some different compositional choices and see how that affects the feel of the drawing.

This time, I'm only making one small change. Rather than placing the figure straight up and down, I'm tipping them to the right, so now they're a little off balance. Suddenly, there are lots of different diagonal lines in the drawing. Do you see how this creates a more dynamic composition? Horizontal and vertical lines can make a composition feel very stable. Diagonal lines can shake things up and create more of a sense of movement.

In this next version, I'm repeating the figure many times and overlapping them as they move into the distance. (I'm following the rules of one-point perspective to get their heights right.) The repetition and overlapping create a sense of rhythm and movement even though the figures are still. Their heads and feet create new diagonal lines that make this composition more dynamic. Also, the meaning of the picture changes. What story do we imagine when we see a lone figure in a vast landscape? How does the narrative change when there are a dozen replicas of the same figure standing in a line?

All of these compositional choices are valid! It's all about the effect you want to achieve.

BASIC COMPOSITION STRUCTURES

One aspect of composition is the underlying structure of the image: it's a basic shape that is formed by the elements of your drawing. Some people call these basic underlying structures "armatures." There are many different armatures in drawing, so I'm just going to show you some of my favorites.

I almost never realize my drawings are using one of these structures until it's all over and I'm looking back over it. You may have fun playing around with these, or it just might be an interesting way to look at the artwork you've already made, to see if your drawings tend toward a specific shape or structure.

Also, if your drawings are very serene and you'd like to try something more active, you could try switching up the basic "shape" that you've organized your drawing into.

1. Triangle

See how this self-portrait by the artist Malvin Gray Johnson uses a triangle shape as its main compositional structure? A triangle with a flat base is a strong, solid shape.

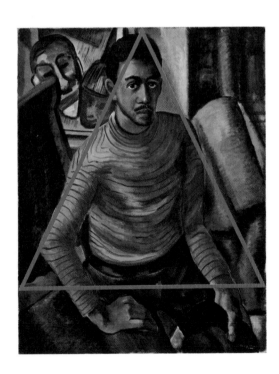

2. "L" Shape

When you look at this portrait by Alice Pike Barney do you get a steady and calm feeling? The torso and lap of the figure form a (backwards) "L" shape.

3. Central Mass

Do you see how the baby and all the bright blankets are gathered into one central mass? I enjoy this structure because it's simple but can also allow you to gather a bunch of different subjects and have them all make sense together in the same space. Even though this is a tiny, fragile newborn child, the artist, Gustav Klimt, places her at the top of the mass, giving her a sense of heft and importance.

These three structures tend to feel more stable and peaceful.

These two structures tend to feel more dynamic and imply motion.

4. "S" Curve

See this relatively simple landscape by painter Edgar Degas? It feels so simple, a grassy field with a little path running through it and a small stretch of cloudy sky in the distance. Yet, I keep finding my eye traveling through the picture and not getting "stuck." The "S" shape that this composition relies on is key to keeping movement in the image.

5. Radiating Lines

This image, also by Degas, gets a lot of its energy from the "radiating lines" that are suggested throughout the picture— from the arm gestures of the central dancer to the energetic folds of the dancers' skirts. See how if you extend these lines outward you see almost star-like bursts of lines radiating off the page?

POINT OF VIEW

Point of view is exactly what it sounds like. It's the point, or place, from which you're viewing your subjects. You can create wildly different effects depending upon the vantage point from which the artist (and therefore the art-viewer) is looking at her subjects.

▲ If you want the subject to feel important or larger-than-life, you can place the point of view below the subject, so the viewer is looking "up at them".

▲ Placing your subject eye-level with the viewer can also create a powerful effect. If your subject is a person, placing them at eye-level can create the feeling of a conversation between the subject and the viewer as equals.

▲ If you want the subject to seem small, or vulnerable for example, it can help to place the point of view above the subject.

POINT OF VIEW AND PROPORTION AND SCALE

Look at these two different drawings. In each, I'm drawing the same subject, a paper boat floating on a puddle. But look how by changing the point of view and proportion and scale I'm able to create two very different experiences of the same subject.

▲ In this first drawing, the point of view is from above the puddle, making the puddle feel smaller, about the size it would be if you encountered it in real life. I chose to keep a little bit of a figure wearing rain boots in the composition, which gives us a point of reference of "relative scale." We know the puddle is regular size, because we see how it relates to another familiar thing that we know the basic size of. So, because of the **point of view** and **proportion** and **scale** of the subjects, the effect of this first drawing is that you are seeing a small paper boat on a regular-size rain puddle.

▲ Now, let's look at this second drawing. First, I changed the point of view so the artist/viewer is almost eye-level with the puddle. This changes the feeling of the piece because it gives the puddle and boat a stronger, more powerful position in the composition. I also zoomed in closer to make the boat feel more monumental. I cropped the boots and other surrounding details out so there's nothing to indicate how large or small the puddle and boat are. Finally, I used the principles of atmospheric perspective (where things in the foreground are sharper and darker, and things in the background are fuzzier and lighter in value) to give the puddle an epic quality.

It's the point of view, proportion and scale, and cropping *choices* that make these compositions have meaning and mood. This is our world. This is our artwork. We get to decide what's important and what's not.

CONTRAST AND VALUE IN COMPOSITION

Check out this image.

▲ See how it feels kind of "blah"? Like it's all sort of gray and washed out? By increasing the **contrast** (the difference between the lightest areas and the darkest areas) we can help "wake up" the drawing.

▲ That's an improvement. By increasing the contrast, we've created a focal point and our eye is drawn to the central figure.

It can also be a good idea to think of your composition in terms of simple shapes of different values. Rather than looking at the actual figures or objects, squint and see the shapes of shadow and light.

SQUINTING

If you ever find yourself struggling to see the different areas of light and dark in your subject or in your drawing, try squinting at it to blur your vision a little. Or, if you wear glasses, take them off!

One of the most powerful tools for seeing the world is squinting. I know this can seem illogical. How could limiting your ability to see help you see better? But squinting is a great way to simplify what you're looking at into its most basic shapes and into its most basic values.

See how this first photo is perfectly in focus, but it's busy. It's not clear what the most important part is. We don't feel the artist showing us what they think is most important, inviting us to examine that more closely.

In this second shot, though we've lost the detail, we can start to see and think in terms of basic shapes and masses of value. From here, we can edit and choose what we want to keep and what to leave out. We can invite the viewer to explore what we find most interesting.

Anytime you're struggling with composition, try to start simple. Squint to see your most important basic shapes and play around with different ways to lay them out on your page.

CHAPTER 7 STYLE

Style is *how* you make your drawing. It's your unique way of making marks and putting a picture together. Your style is your artistic signature.

Though style can be a hard thing to pin down, you know it when you see it. You may have a favorite artist whose work you recognize whether you've seen it before or not. Because you're familiar with their unique style.

There are many things that influence an artist's style, including quality of line, medium (what you draw with), surface (what you draw on), format (size and shape of your surface), artistic instincts (what you naturally like), and artistic influences (other artists' work you like). Let's explore.

QUALITY OF LINE

In drawing, the way you make your marks has a huge effect on your style. Many different things add up to an artist's particular style, but in drawing few things are as important as how you lay down your actual marks. Are they bold and heavy? Are they light and delicate? Are they quick? Are they slow and steady? Most of us have a natural, intuitive way of moving our hand around the page. Just like when we are quickly writing down a note, our handwriting has its own natural personality.

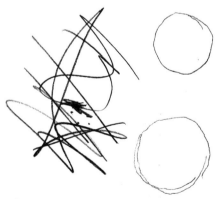

◀ A simple mark can communicate a lot. Can you draw a line that is angry? Timid? In a hurry? Sad? Excited?

77

There are many different techniques artists choose when making their marks. Here are a few:

▶ Hatching

In this Leonardo da Vinci sketch, the artist uses "hatching" to make the shadows. Rather than making smooth marks to make the mid-tone gray for the shadows, he makes little parallel straight lines or "hatch" marks to create the shadow.

▶ Pointillism

In this piece, Paul Signac didn't draw any actual lines. Instead, the artist made thousands of little dots to draw the figures and the scene. In darker areas, he concentrated the dots closer together, in lighter areas, he drew them farther apart.

▶ Bold, Expressive Lines

Rembrandt uses bold, dark lines to render this figure. You can feel the quickness of his hand in his marks. The figure is curved over and there is a heaviness to her pose. The bold lines deepen this sense of weightiness.

EXPLORE STYLE MOVEMENTS

There are a couple of ways we can look at style. There's your specific style as an individual artist, and there are also different style movements throughout art history. Historical style movements are when a group of artists explored and developed a specific style of art around the same time. You may find yourself drawn to one or more of these styles. Exploring style movements can be a great source of inspiration and can help you develop and shape your own personal style. There are many major style movements, so I'm just going to share a few of my favorites:

▶ Expressionism

Expressionism is a style characterized by bold and free mark-making. It is less concerned with precision and more concerned with expressing a particular emotional tone or energy. I drew this self-portrait in the style of Käthe Kollwitz, after her *Self-Portrait, Drawing*, 1933. Her drawings are a beautiful example of expressionism. The arm, which is in constant movement as the artist draws, is represented through a giant, bold scribble, made with the broad edge of a piece of charcoal. You can feel the energy of the artist's arm coursing through the line that represents it.

▶ Realism

Realism is a style that celebrates the normal, everyday parts of life. Here the artist Charles Demuth rendered a bunch of beautiful pears and an overturned bowl. For you, it might mean drawing a picture of your almost-empty cereal bowl after breakfast, your dog resting by the sofa, or your friend while they do their homework.

▶ Surrealism

I drew this in the style of Remedios Varo, Spanish surrealist who lived most of her adult life in Mexico. It is a reinterpretation of her drawing *La Creación de Los Aves (The Creation of the Birds)*. The word *Surrealism* came from a French word meaning "beyond what is real." Surrealist artworks involve closely observed subjects from life, but things can happen in these pictures that are above and beyond the rules that govern reality. So a hummingbird can live in an empty place in a figure's chest. And a person can be evolving into an owl-like bird. The spaces in Surrealist artwork are often eerie and mysterious.

▶ Trompe l'Oeil/ Hyperrealism

For hundreds of years, there have been artists obsessed with rendering what they see with as much lifelike detail as possible. In the 1600s this technique came to be called "Trompe l'Oeil," which is French for "fool the eye." The finished drawing is so precise that the viewer might wonder whether it is in fact a drawing or a photograph. It blows my mind an artist named Cornelius Norbertus Gijsbrechts painted this over 350 years ago.

▶ Cubism

Cubism is a school of style in which the artist seems to look at and represent the subject from many different angles at the same time like in this self-portrait by Reijer Stolk. It gives the subject a fragmented, dynamic quality.

EXPLORING THE EXTREMES OF STYLE

▶ Hyperrealism

If you find yourself drawn to realism or even photorealism and are struggling to capture your subject as "accurately" as you want, a great tool to use is gridding. Throughout art history, artists have used different tools to help them find the shape and form of their subjects. Even before modern cameras were invented, some artists used technologies that helped them project and trace their subjects! So, it's absolutely okay to use any technologies or tricks that help you achieve the art you want to achieve.

Pick a printed photo to work from that will hold your attention. Achieving this kind of detail and heightened realism takes some time. Ideally, pick a photograph that's okay to draw directly on—not one that is a precious treasure. If you can't find one you can freely draw on, draw the grid on a piece of plastic and lay that grid over the photo and carefully tape it from behind so you don't damage the photo. Another option is to find a photo in an old magazine you can draw directly on.

▶ Gridding How-to

1. Use a ruler to draw a grid on your photograph. I made mine 9 inches across and 8 inches down.

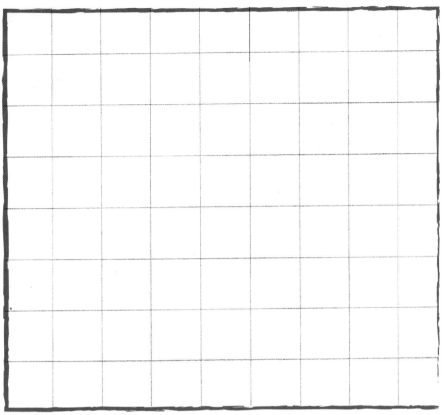

2. Draw a grid with the exact same number of squares on a piece of paper. I made mine the exact same size as the grid on my photo. If you want a larger drawing than your photograph, you could make each of the squares on your paper 2 inches instead of 1 inch.

3. Going square by square with a number 2 pencil, draw the lines and shapes you see. It is easier to get a likeness this way than by just trying to draw the whole face all at once. You're breaking this complex face down to manageable little shapes. Don't worry about value at this point. Just basic lines and shapes.

4. Now try to find the areas of different values. Squinting can help if you're having a hard time seeing them. Draw the "shapes" that mark areas of mid-gray, highlights, and dark shadows. Your figure may look a little cartoonish and strange at this stage.

5. Use your eraser to soften the outlines of the shapes you just drew and begin sketching in the shadows.

6. Now it's time to soften the grid and all the outlines of the shadow shapes with your eraser. Pay attention to the lighter gray values in the figure's skin tone. Sketch them in, keeping the highlight areas bright. Notice the transitions between light tones, mid-tones, and dark grays.

7. Next erase the remaining grid lines. Block in the medium and dark tones in her hair. And begin adding some darker grays to the details of her face.

Tip on drawing teeth: notice how the "lines" between the teeth aren't hard edges at all. They're areas of shaded light gray. Dark lines tend to make teeth look like comical doll teeth.

8. I've only used a number 2 pencil at this point. Now it's time to use one of the darker pencils to draw the darker areas of hair, and the darker details on her face (eyes, corners of her mouth). And go back through her face and neck with a number 2 pencil to deepen shadows and adjust the transitions from shadow to light on her cheeks.

9. For this final pass, deepen your darkest darks. Refine your details. Use your eraser to pull out highlights in areas that may have gotten a little smudgy during the process.

USE TIME LIMITS TO DRAW MORE FREELY

Now, let's explore the other end of the drawing spectrum. Set a timer for 1 hour and draw the same image you just drew through gridding. How does this change your drawing?

Now set a timer for 2 minutes! How does this change your drawing? Is it looser and less detailed? Are the lines bolder? More expressive?

I once had a professor who gave us the assignment to make 50 drawings of the same subject and they were due the next day. I panicked. My drawing style was slow and deliberate, and it would be impossible to make 50 decent drawings in time for our next class. After the fifth drawing, I realized I had to change my approach to finish on time. I had a creative breakthrough! I started making big, loose sketchy lines. I did a drawing in five minutes! The next one I did in thirty seconds! I was loosening up and having fun! My teacher reminded me how to play by giving such a difficult assignment. By the time I got to the 50th drawing, it was almost completely abstract. I'd explored the range from detailed realism to abstract expressionism overnight!

Be free! Let it be messy! Let go of the concern about it looking like something or being "pretty"!

CHAPTER 8

YOUR "WHAT"

What are you drawn to draw? Finding your "what" may be easy. You may want to draw face after face after face. You may know that you love more than anything to draw fantasy pictures of winged creatures launching from the branches of trees. Or, if you're like a lot of artists, you may find yourself saying "I don't know what to draw." Any one of those things is okay.

If you're in the first group, and you know just what you're drawn to draw, you can use these exercises to stretch and expand your personal cast of characters. If you're in the second group, you can use them to start to get a feel for what you're more interested in exploring. Either way, your journey as an artist (and the "content," the *what* of your drawings) will change and grow over time, just like you do.

Look to your life! Your unique, lived experience is another path to finding your *what*. Your experience matters! Anyone old enough to read this book knows life isn't always easy. Sometimes it's great and fun and beautiful. And sometimes life is hard. Sometimes very hard. You can put all that into your artwork too.

You may need to search. What you need to express may not be obvious to you right away. You may need to do some digging to find what's below the surface.

I've been drawing for a very long time, and there are some subjects that have captured my attention for as long as I can remember (people, books, the insides of buildings and rooms) and many other things that I've become interested in exploring over time. By now, I've got a pretty long list of what I like to look at and revisit over and over again. You know what's amazing? I discover new ways of seeing them *all the time.* Somehow, I still *never expect to,* and I always find it surprising. But drawing the world is amazing like that.

I've always loved drawing interior spaces—the insides of buildings and houses and imaginary structures. I think it's because I grew up around lots of old buildings. My mom worked on old houses throughout my childhood, so I often found myself in old, high-ceilinged houses with giant, heavy wooden doors and enormous, tall windows. I loved the way the low winter sun poured in through those antique windows and stretched dramatic rectangles of light across the worn wooden floors. While my mom was sanding floors and repairing windows, I was absorbing all those images and filing them away. Years later I found myself drawing and painting figures inside these mysterious old spaces with light flooding through doorways and windows.

DEVELOPING YOUR UNIQUE CAST OF CHARACTERS

Begin keeping a list of things you notice that you like to draw. Here are some questions that might help you land on new subjects to try. Remember, nothing is hard and fast. Everything can change. If something occurs to you, just try it.

▶ Ask Yourself

- Where do you live?
- Is there anything about the place you live you find interesting? A view out your window? What do you see when you look out your door? Do you live in the city? Country? Suburbs? A house? An apartment?
- What are your favorite things to do or to look at, even if you can't explain why?
- What do you like to do? Kick a ball? Climb trees?
- Are you obsessed with your cat?
- Do you have favorite themes you like to daydream about? (Flying, fairies, myths, slides, twisty forever staircases?)
- What is unique to your past? Is there anything from back then that could make its way into your art now?
- What do you imagine about your future? Is there any part of this that you could draw into being on your paper?
- How do you feel? Are you bright and energized? Are you sluggish and worn out? Any of these can be good launching points for a drawing. In fact, when life is hard, when we're in a bad mood, or feel sad, lonely or isolated, it can be an especially rich time to draw . . . to "get it out" whatever "it" is, onto the paper.

USING THE "BAD" STUFF TO MAKE GOOD ART

The incredible artist Louise Bourgeois made her entire career out of studying fear. She created giant spiders and all kinds of abstract and representational objects that reflected a kind of panic and terror. It took a lot of courage and strength to delve so deeply into content that made her uncomfortable. It was this deep, mysterious stuff that fed her art-making life for 70+ years!

▶ Try This

Make a list of subjects you dislike or are even repulsed by. Sometimes what scares us or makes us uncomfortable can be really "juicy" material for our artwork.

For example, I once lived in a house with a really creepy basement. The ceiling was so low I had to shorten my easel so it would fit down there, and I set it up among the spiderwebs and hair-raising insects with a thousand tiny legs. I painted a couple paintings of that spooky basement that I wound up really loving.

This is one of those old paintings. I painted it in that dank basement with the cellar door to the outside cracked. I used an old black-and-white family photo from 1941 for the face and shoulders of the little girl and imagined the rest. This is the kind of thing we're going to do more of in Chapter 10. We're going to use several different sources (in this case a place observed from real life, a photograph, and my imagination) in the same composition to make our own world come to life.

PROJECT | Invent a New Character

Use your creative eye to invent a couple new characters to add to your "what" collection.

Person + Animal =

Find a photo of someone you'd like to draw and then either a photograph of an animal, a stuffed animal, or a pet that's a good sport and is willing to model for you. I knew I wanted to draw my daughter with the wings of a hawk. I'd never drawn a hawk before. I've drawn countless human figures, but not a lot of birds, and definitely no hawks. So I decided that to get my person-animal creature the way I wanted, I needed to do some hawk "studies." That's where you just look at the new subject closely and do lots of little sketches to learn more about how it's structured. Here are a few sketches from my sketchbook.

Next I chose some images to work from to capture the human and the hawk. Here's what I came up with. Now you try it with your own person and animal combo!

**Random Inanimate Object +
Random Inanimate Object =**

Find two relatively simple objects lying around your house. Now, use them to create a new life form.

EMBRACE YOUR LIMITATIONS TO FIND YOUR "WHAT"

The combination of your skills and your limitations is what makes your art interesting. Don't be afraid of those places that you feel really challenged by as an artist.

Maybe the particular way you distort a favorite subject when you draw it is exactly what makes your drawing unusual. Or maybe you love drawing people but don't enjoy drawing faces. No problem! Pull their hat down, or let their hair blow across their face. You can always continue to build your skills, and you can also embrace your limitations to create images that are unique to you.

If you're still searching for your content, your special "what," that's great! Stay open! Stay curious! Explore, explore, explore!

CHAPTER 9 YOUR "HOW": DEVELOPING YOUR UNIQUE STYLE

Style is your personal signature. Your fingerprint. Your you-and-only-you way of doing things. It might not be easy to identify at first because you're trying new things. But you're leaving your artistic DNA on the page whether you intend to or not. There's something unmistakable and unique about every person's way of laying down a line, their way of seeing the world. You can make choices about your personal style, and there are also aspects of your style that choose you. It's sort of like your speaking voice: there is a range of notes and tones and volumes you can use to express yourself, but they are all still aspects of your one and only voice. And, just like your voice, it will evolve and change over time.

EMBRACE YOUR LIMITATIONS TO FIND YOUR "HOW"

An artist's style often boils down to a combination of their skills AND (no less important) their *limitations*. Style can be the unique combo of your aspirations (what you imagine/hope to create) and limitations (the ways your artwork maybe doesn't quite match the idea you had in your head). There can be a tension here that can be a good and creative thing. There are lots of well-known artists who never quite felt that what they created matched their vision. But that strange, mysterious combination of their strengths and imperfections is what made their work so special.

Phil Hansen is a contemporary artist who used to make realistic, pointillist artwork. He developed a tremor and his shaky hand could no longer deliver the surgical precision onto his drawing paper that it could before. He thought his art career was over . . . until he met a doctor who asked him why he didn't just "embrace the shake." It was a breakthrough. By accepting this new limitation as a quality of his artwork, he opened a whole new world of creativity.

I drew these in the style of Phil Hansen.

Frida Kahlo was a painter who suffered severe injuries in a bus accident when she was young. That trauma informed the "what" and "how" of her artwork for the rest of her life. She painted self-portraits that made her emotional and physical pain visible. When she was recovering from one of many surgeries, she would have a canvas suspended above her bed so she could still paint.

At first this might feel frustrating . . . the thought of accepting your life struggles as part of your art. But for the aspects of our lives that are truly outside our control, this might be the most creative thing we can do.

And if you've got frustrations with your artistic "shortcomings," don't worry—you can always continue to work on developing your skills and getting more competent in the areas where you're struggling. But there can also be a lot of freedom in embracing your imperfections as an artist. Sometimes your struggles are part of what makes you and your artwork interesting.

WHAT'S GOING ON IN YOUR LIFE CAN AFFECT YOUR STYLE

Here's something I've noticed about my own artwork when I look back at different periods of my life: when I've been in a really confident, dynamic place in my life, my paintings have often been fast, bold, painterly, and active. When I've been in a more challenging place in my life, my paintings have been quiet, soft, with more careful and deliberate brushstrokes.

Both of those dynamics have produced some good (and bad! That's useful too!) work. You don't have to be in a big, happy, bold time in your life to make beautiful art. Sometimes good artwork can come from a more difficult or even painful place.

The key is that art needs your heart to be open to whatever you're experiencing. Only then can your creative spark and your imagination monster fully express themselves.

See this dreamy image? The famous artist Albrecht Dürer created it in 1925 after he awoke from a nightmare. He dreamt that there was a violent rainstorm.

Can you see how loose and free his marks are? He lets the paint drip and spread unconstrained down the page. You may be surprised to learn that Dürer's typical style, the style for which he is most well-known, is highly controlled and detailed. In fact, I couldn't have guessed in a million years that this small painting was by Albrecht Dürer if his name hadn't been written right next to it. Check out what one of his pieces in his "typical" style looks like:

This image is so detailed you can see the individual hairs of the rabbit. His style is realistic, exacting, and has hard edges. The shock of the nightmare shook loose all of his typical artistic habits and inclinations. In the dream image, the edges are soft and free. His emotional state completely transformed his style.

USE YOUR "WHAT" TO FIND YOUR "HOW"—AN EXPERIMENT

Draw something you LOVE:

How does drawing something you really, really love affect your style? I find if I'm drawing something (or especially someone—like my child or friend or family member) I get a little more tight. I'm so invested in communicating the beauty of the person as they are in the world, and getting the likeness just right, that I clam up a little. It's a tendency I've learned I need to be aware of.

Draw something you DISLIKE or have negative feelings about:

How does drawing something you don't have a lot of affection for affect the way you draw? I find drawing something I dislike actually helps me move the pencil a little more freely.

You know what's funny? After drawing a subject, I usually find I like it a lot more than I thought I did.

Draw something you feel NEUTRAL about:

How does this affect the way you approach your
drawing? I find it actually gives me a sense of freedom.
I'm not as attached to the outcome, so I can just "take my
pencil for a walk" around the page and let myself explore this
object I may never have paid much attention to. The hilarious
riddle is that when I don't really care if I capture a likeness, my
drawing often winds up being more of a precise representation of the subject
than when I am really trying hard.

  A wise friend of mine once told me that if my hands are gripped in fists, they
won't be open to receive all the beauty and gifts life has to offer. Of course that was
meant as a metaphor, but the same can be said for drawing, even quite literally. If our grip
is a little softer, if our intention is relaxed, we can get into that sweet spot where things just kind
of flow, and we're not exerting our will over the page as much.

EXPLORE YOUR NATURAL STYLISTIC PREFERENCES

It can be helpful to explore and understand your instinctive
way of making drawings. You may want to always stay with
these preferences, but if you know what they are, you can have
the choice to intentionally change things up if you want to.

  Ask yourself:

  What is my natural way of making marks on the
page, my "quality of line"? Is it loose, tight, heavy, soft,
quick, careful, fast, slow? Do I make small, jagged
marks? Or do I prefer long, swoopy pencil lines?

  Am I drawn to a particular school of style?
Are my drawings mostly realistic? Do I want to
push that and make them more realistic? Or do I
want to make them sketchier? Or more abstract?

EXPERIMENT WITH SCALE AND FORMAT

▶ Your Drawing Surface, Your Scale

Scale is another word for size. It can refer to the size of your paper, or the size of the subjects in your drawing.

There are some artists, for example, whose works are very easily recognizable not just because they are known for drawing or painting certain subjects, but because they're known to do them on gigantic surfaces. Or, they're known for taking relatively small subjects and zooming in on them to make them huge.

See how different the effect is when you make different choices about scale?

The scale of your drawing can be a powerful way to define your style. A drawing that is 3 inches wide and 4 inches tall is going to feel dramatically different from a drawing that is 3 feet wide and 4 feet tall.

Experiment with the Scale of your Drawing:

Try drawing one of your favorite subjects on a tiny piece of paper.

Now try it on a large piece of paper. If you don't have a giant piece of drawing paper, tape several pieces of paper together, or draw on a large piece of cardboard.

Experiment with the Scale of your Subject:

Pick an object. Now draw it so that it's much smaller than life size. How does that affect the feeling of the artwork?

Now draw it so it's much larger than life size. What different effect does this have?

▶ **Format**

Unusual Shapes:

You may find that you enjoy breaking with the more conventional shapes. Maybe you are attracted to the idea of drawing on circles.

Perhaps you want to draw on a shape that is very short and very wide.

I once sewed 53 pieces of paper together so that I could make a short and verrry wide drawing. It was only 6 inches tall but 185 inches wide!

EXPERIMENT WITH MEDIUM AND SURFACE

You can explore your style range by playing around drawing with different supplies on different surfaces. Your medium of choice (pencil, chalk, char-coal, pen) will influence the look of your artwork. What you choose to draw on (conventional white paper vs. an old book page or paper sack) will also affect your style.

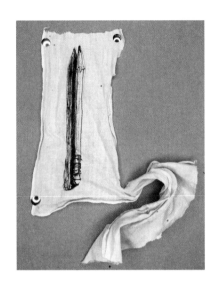

▲ I drew this drawing with a black felt tip pen on a torn up old cloth napkin I found in the rag drawer. I used thumb tacks to attach it to a piece of cardboard while I was drawing. It was a fun change to draw on a wrinkly surface that "fought" my pen and made it impossible to draw a truly straight line.

▲ Here I experimented with drawing on a "toned" surface (it's a medium gray-brown shoe-box lid rather than the typical bright white of paper), and I drew my darks and lights with black and white colored pencils.

YOUR INFLUENCES

Take plenty of time looking at other people's art. If you have access to an art museum in your town or city, see if you can make a trip! If not, I've always loved checking out giant art books from the library.

All the art we love (music, painting, dance) draws from and builds on art that came before it. Whether we're aware of our influences or not, they are there. Just like people grow and change and live in rela-tion to one another, art grows and changes in conversation with other art! By exploring other artists, you learn more about yourself as an artist.

YOUR WORLD

Are you ready to use everything you've learned so far to bring your world into existence? In this chapter I'm going to show you how to use all the tools you've acquired to bring your vision to life. We're going to use all our favorite different subjects and our favorite places/scapes to build a world.

We're going to use everything we know about light and shadow and composition to make all these different pieces work together in the same place.

You can use a photo, a favorite object, and a character from your imagination all in the same worldscape.

▲ For this drawing, I used a box room (Chapter 5), a paper boat (Chapter 4), and a couple of source photos for the figures' faces.

I placed the paper boat in the box room and adjusted my table lamp until I loved the way the light spilled over the boat and onto the "floor."

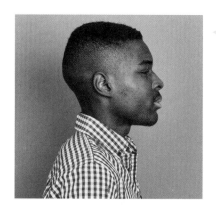

I knew I wanted two figures in profile (from the side), and I had these two beautiful photos of people's faces, but I didn't have any reference photos with the figures in the right pose. So, I sat down on the floor next to a mirror. I drew my knees toward me and looked in the mirror to get a sense of what this pose would look like. I combined these faces and what I was able to sketch from my own body in the mirror to draw the figures in this scene. I didn't need them to have a lot of detail, but I wanted to reference photographs for the faces so they felt more real than if I'd just drawn them from my imagination. Finally, I imagined the way the light would illuminate their faces and tops of their arms, while the backs of their bodies and sides of their bodies opposite the window would be in shadow.

For this drawing, I used a book and two reference photos: one of some waves and one of a child in overalls sitting at the end of a dock.

I had originally pictured the figure differently, but I found this photo of this kid sitting in exactly the pose I'd imagined, so I went ahead and drew her pretty much as she was. I just adjusted the position of her face.

First, I drew the book from observation. Then I "cut out" the pool area in the center of the book using my imagination and what

I know about one-point perspective. For the top and bottom lines, I followed the curves of the pages. For the right and left sides of the pool, I drew the lines so they point to the same vanishing point that the sides of the book do. Then I sketched in the figure and the waves. I don't have a lot of experience drawing waves, so that was a fun experiment. I found myself laying down lots of layers of value and then using my eraser (as we did with the cloud in Chapter 4) to "lift" some sparkly highlights on the waves.

The light source in my picture is coming from behind the child and the book, so the cast shadows fall toward the viewer. I'm using different source references for my drawing, but I'm thinking about how the light falls over everything in a similar way so they seem like they're part of the same space.

This drawing is almost entirely from my imagination, except
for a spool of thread and a marble on my table for reference.
The rest is made up of basic shapes (tubes and a box for the
castle) and a simplified figure (with a spherical marble skirt).
I imagined at least two different light sources and drew the
shadows accordingly. These multiple light sources would make
no logical sense in the real world, but they felt right to me in
my world. Your world, your rules.

USE A FAMOUS COMPOSITION WITH YOUR "WHAT" AND "HOW":

Materials you'll need for this project:

- A picture of an artist's work you like

- Your drawing materials

I chose a famous painting by Johannes Vermeer called *Woman Reading a Letter*. I love the L-shaped composition, the strong central figure with her delicate gesture holding the letter, and the way the light falls across her and the room around her.

Here's the scene as I see it: the young man is reading a message on his phone. Like Vermeer's figure, he is having an intimate moment of solitude, reading a message from a loved one, his hands in a similar gentle gesture, holding his phone. You may recognize this figure from Chapter 3.

I drew much simpler chairs that feel more contemporary than the ones in the painting. The light streams over the table and across the figure. In the background, instead of an old-fashioned tapestry, I drew a painting in the style of the pioneering abstract painter Alma Thomas.

Art is a mysterious process, and none of us arrive to it truly knowing what we're doing. Have you ever heard that running is just "a controlled fall"? That when we move our bodies forward quickly, we're basically just stringing together a relatively graceful series of stumbles and trips? We're simply keeping ourselves from falling on our faces one footfall at a time.

That's sort of what we're doing when we make art. We're hurtling ourselves forward into the unknown and onto our page. We try some things, and they work. Our foot lands and supports us just before we fall. Other times we try something and it doesn't work; we may even fall on our faces. But all of that is good. All of it is creatively useful. You can't experiment without making a mess. And you can't learn without experimentation.

Don't worry if your artwork doesn't turn out *exactly* how you imagined it. Who knows? Your unique artistic contribution might be exactly the thing that's not quite what you pictured in your head—that rich place between what you hope to create and what your hand, eyes, and skill set actually bring to life on paper.

Trust yourself and your process, and keep trying new things. Keep stumbling into the unknown of your creative journey, trusting that you are learning and growing every step of the way.

▶ Linear Perspective Refresher

We explored linear perspective in *Art for Kids: Drawing*, but it comes in handy throughout this book too. So, here's a little refresher for those of you who haven't used it in a while.

Parallel lines seem to get closer together the farther away they are. They appear to come together in the distance at an invisible spot called the "vanishing point." This illusion is extremely useful to artists because it gives us some "rules" for creating a sense of depth and space in our drawings when we're drawing things with square edges like rooms and buildings.

One-Point Perspective

In one-point perspective, you've got three basic parts:

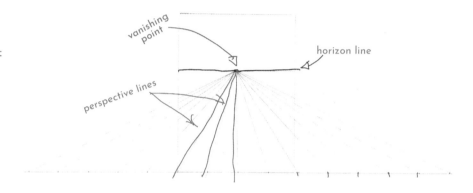

Here we're going to use one-point perspective to draw a checkered floor.

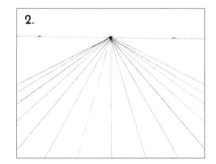

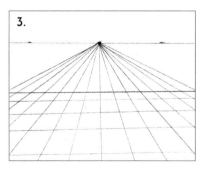

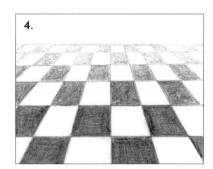

Two-Point Perspective

The difference between one-point and two-point perspective is—you guessed it—a second vanishing point!

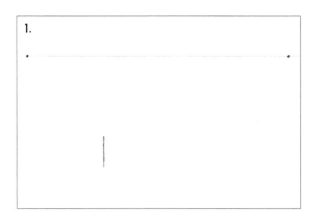

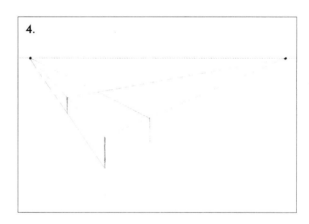

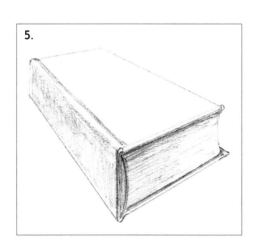

▶ Advanced Shading

When light falls over an object, it creates all kinds of interesting shadows and highlights. Each of these shades— from dark black to bright white—is called a value. Identifying the values in your subjects is what's going to give your drawings dimension and depth.

We explored light and shadow in *Art for Kids: Drawing*, and here we're going to take it a little further.

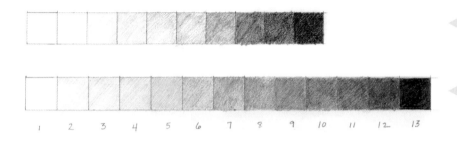

To refresh, these are value scales.

See how it goes from dark to light, with each shade of value in between an even "step" from the one before it. There are ten different values in the first value scale. Can you draw a similar series of boxes and practice finding the shades from light to dark?

Now let's try it again but with more boxes. Now we're searching for even more values, teaching our eyes to distinguish more subtle differences in value.

ACKNOWLEDGMENTS

It takes a lot of people to make a book.

I am deeply grateful to these people for all the hours and energy they poured into this project:

Ardi Alspach, an exceptional editor, who understood the spirit of this book from the beginning and was able to give it the magical balance of space and structure it needed to find its shape.

Julie Robine, a brilliant designer, who brought all her talents (including her eye as an artist and illustrator) into the design of the book. I so appreciated knowing this material was in the hands of a designer with such a breadth of skill and understanding.

Scott Amerman, managing editor, who kept his arms around the big picture of this book so the rest of us could get lost in the weeds (an essential part of the process!) without losing our way.

And to the rest of the Union Square Kids team who invested their gifts into bringing this project to life.

I'd also like to thank:

Debra Kass Orenstein for her invaluable professional guidance.

And the original team at Lark Books (Asheville's once-upon-a-time small press) who launched Art for Kids: Drawing into the universe: Joe Rhatigan and Rain Newcomb, editors, and Celia Naranjo, designer.

The Authors Guild

I'm eternally grateful to all the artists and teachers who have patiently (and sometimes impatiently) taught me over the years:

Sylvia Boyd, John Payne, Adele Wayman, Mike Northius, Roy Nydorf, Jane Sibley, Nina Alan, Barbara Grossman, Judy Glantzman, Bob Godfrey, Elena Sisto

Jeanine Siler Jones, for teaching me to compost the hard stuff into the soil so it can nourish whatever is ready to grow and blossom.

The whole Maybin family for loving me and Lyme (and now Palmer) like family these past twenty years.

Ms. Ruby Maybin, who teaches us that there are no do-overs in life and to dance as much as we can while our bodies still cooperate.

Mike Maybin, who has the most soul-healing laugh and is a genius of alchemy: he knows how to transform the pain of life into an irrepressible urgency to savor every bit of beauty the moment has to offer.

Bruce McConnel for capturing "Puppy Tree" at her cutest and for being a fellow family traveler along the artist's path.

Karen Biel Kelly for her photography, ebullient encouragement, and friendship.

June Kelly for being an inspired and inspiring artist and for being game to model for the book.

Mom and Dad, who have been making and creating as long as I can remember: Dad with words and thoughts, and Mom with every other conceivable medium (cloth, iron, paint, construction materials, side-of-the-road trash, etc.).

Joe Dagnese for friendship, love, and guidance, and for setting an example for how to kick out the writing jams under pressure and how to live a cleverly diversified creative life.

Denise Kiernan for friendship, love, and guidance, and for showing me how to step into unapologetic creative power.

Lizzy and Hans for being my fresh eyes on drawings I've looked at far too long.

My beautiful community of friends and neighbors who have made two very challenging years on earth an opportunity for deepened connection.

This book wouldn't exist without my partner Lyme, who is my trusted sounding board for every new idea, my first reader, and my first editor.

Thanks to my partner and child who give me the gift of seeing the world through their attentive, sensitive eyes every day. I love you with all my heart forever.

Resources

If you're interested in further instruction in composition, Molly Bang and Ian Roberts are experts.

Shaun Tan's *The Bird King: An Artist's Notebook* is a beautiful book. An artist revealing their creative process.

All of Austin Kleon's books on creativity will help free you up, especially *Show Your Work!*

All of Lynda Barry's work is a giant permission slip to be your own, beautiful, weird creative self.

All images by Kathryn Temple except for the following:

Art Institute of Chicago: Gift of Dorothy Braude Edinburg to the Harry B. and Bessie K. Braude Memorial Collection: 71 top

Getty Images: E+: Andrew_Howe: 78 bottom; iStock/Getty Images Plus: Ailime: 4 (pencils); ImagePixel: 4 (kneaded eraser); Mooikunst: cover and throughout (splatter); GalapagosFame 4 (white eraser)

Courtesy of Karen Kelly: 12

Courtesy of Bruce McConnel: 7 top left

Metropolitan Museum of Art: Bequest of Mrs. Harry Payne Bingham, 1986: 71 bottom; Robert Lehman Collection, 1975: 78 top

National Gallery of Denmark: 81 top

National Gallery of Art: Gift of Otto and Franziska Kallir with the help of the Carol and Edwin Gaines Fullinwider Fund: 70 bottom

Rijksmuseum: 81 bottom, 109

Shutterstock.com: Africa Studio: 9 top; anahtiris: 54; AndreyCherkasov: 35; Baevskiy Dmitry: 48; Tatyana Bakul: 106 bottom; Chatham172: 106 middle; Fab_1: 14; Gaus: 28; Kevin George: 25 middle left; Oleksii Gerasevych: 76; han871111: 25 top left; kalavati: 33; Elena karetnikova: 8; Jesus Keller: 25 top right; Krakenimages.com: 105 middle; Ivan Kruk: 25 middle right; Lim Yong Hian: 58; mimage-photography: 32 top, 82; ModernNomads: 32 bottom; mvc_stock: 80; NewAfrica: 41; noomcpk: 25 bottom; Potanna: 60; Prostock-studio: 105 bottom; ra2 studio: 19; S-Photo: 106 bottom; Diego Thomazini: 52; TobagoCays: 44; vivasis: 38

Smithsonian American Art Museum: 70 top; Gift of Harmon Foundation: 69

Courtesy of Wikimedia Commons: Albertine Vienna: 98 bottom; Kroller-Muller Museum: 78 middle; Kunsthistorisches Museum: 98 top

Yale University Art Gallery: 80 top